ALTERNATOR
BOOKS™

SPACE IN ACTION

T0373976

SPACE GEAR IN ACTION

An AUGMENTED REALITY Experience

Rebecca E. Hirsch

Lerner Publications ◆ Minneapolis

EXPLORE SPACE IN BRAND-NEW WAYS WITH AUGMENTED REALITY!

1. Ask a parent or guardian for permission to download the free Lerner AR app on your digital device by going to the App Store or Google Play.

2. As you read, look for this icon throughout the book. It means there is an augmented reality experience on that page!

3. Use the Lerner AR app to scan the picture near the icon.

4. Watch space come alive with augmented reality!

CONTENTS

INTRODUCTION
SUITING UP

On March 21, 2019, two NASA astronauts prepared for a **space walk**. Inside the International Space Station (ISS), they put on white **space suits**. They strapped on caps with built-in microphones to communicate with each other and mission controllers on Earth. Then the astronauts put on clear, plastic helmets.

Astronauts get into their space suits with the help of at least one other person.

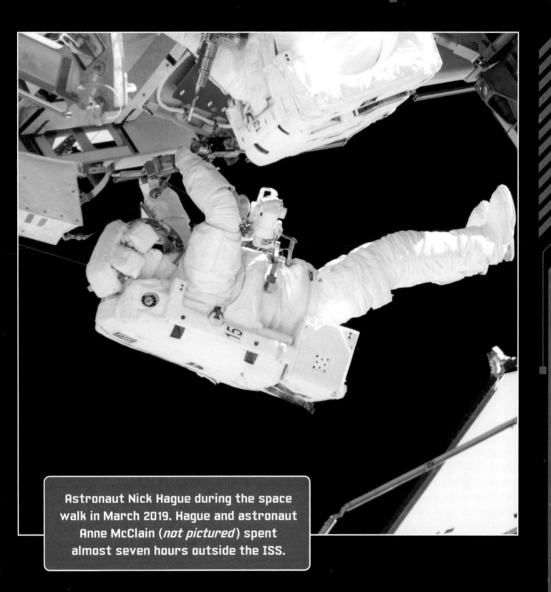

Astronaut Nick Hague during the space walk in March 2019. Hague and astronaut Anne McClain (*not pictured*) spent almost seven hours outside the ISS.

A space suit is like a miniature spacecraft. When the astronauts stepped into space, their suits acted as personal life-support systems. The astronauts used tools and other gear attached to the space suits to replace batteries for the space station's solar panels.

CHAPTER 1

EVOLUTION OF THE SPACE SUIT

I f you stepped into space without a space suit, you would pass out with no oxygen to breathe. Your blood would boil from the lack of **air pressure**, and you would face extreme temperatures. Outside the ISS, it can be 250°F (121°C) in sunlight and -250°F (-156°C) in the shade.

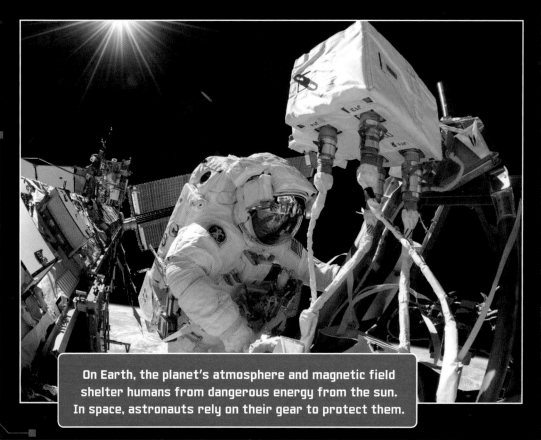

On Earth, the planet's atmosphere and magnetic field shelter humans from dangerous energy from the sun. In space, astronauts rely on their gear to protect them.

A space suit's batteries and oxygen supply are designed to last for almost nine hours.

Space suits are **pressurized** and have breathable oxygen. Layers of fabric maintain an astronaut's temperature and protect her from **radiation** and tiny particles traveling at high speeds. The suits also allow astronauts to see clearly and move easily in space.

EARLY SPACE SUITS

NASA first sent astronauts to space during the Mercury program (1958–1963). Each silver space suit had laced boots, gloves, and a helmet. An oxygen hose attached the suit to the spacecraft. The Mercury astronauts didn't go on space walks, but the suits could be pressurized in an emergency if the pressure in the spacecraft dropped.

On May 5, 1961, Alan Shepard (*top left*) became the first US astronaut to fly to space, soaring 116 miles (186 km) above Earth.

NASA's Gemini program (1961–1966) tested the skills and gear astronauts would need to land on the moon. During space walks, Gemini suits attached to the spacecraft by a hose, which supplied oxygen and cooled the astronauts. But the suits were difficult to move in, and the cooling system didn't always work. Astronauts would get too hot, and their helmets often fogged up.

Edward H. White II took photos with the camera in his right hand on June 3, 1965, during the first space walk for a US astronaut.

Apollo space suits went through extensive testing on Earth before astronauts wore them in space.

APOLLO SPACE SUITS

The Apollo program (1969–1972) sent astronauts to the moon for the first time. Apollo space suits had to work both in the spacecraft and on the lunar surface. They were more flexible than previous suits, allowing astronauts more movement.

To walk on the moon's rough surface, astronauts wore protective boots. A visor shielded their eyes from sunlight. A backpack supplied oxygen, removed **carbon dioxide** that the astronauts exhaled, and helped keep them cool. The Apollo space suit and backpack weighed 180 pounds (82 kg) on Earth, but in the moon's low gravity, the suit weighed only 30 pounds (14 kg).

An astronaut salutes the US flag in 1972 during the final Apollo mission to the moon.

CHAPTER 2

MODERN SPACE SUITS

I t's time for a space walk. First, you pull on a tight-fitting body covering. Water flows through tubes in the garment to help regulate your temperature. Then you wriggle into the two-piece space suit, starting with the heavy pants. A hard shell covers your upper body, while soft, movable sleeves and gloves cover your arms and hands. On your head goes a fabric cap and a plastic helmet with a visor coated in a thin layer of gold to filter the sun's rays. The visor has headlamps and a video camera too.

The space suit's fabric cap contains earphones and microphones.

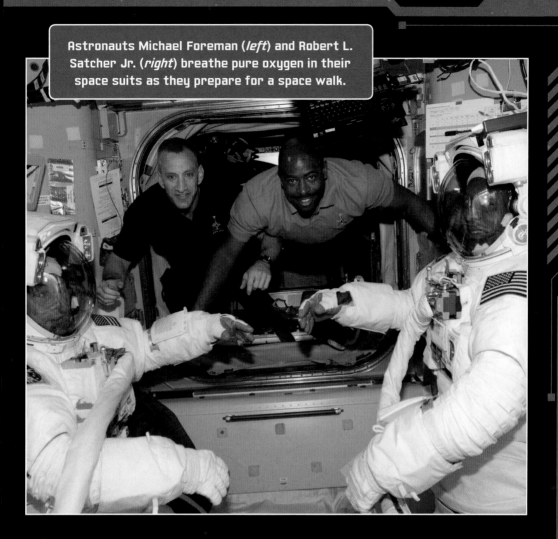

Astronauts Michael Foreman (*left*) and Robert L. Satcher Jr. (*right*) breathe pure oxygen in their space suits as they prepare for a space walk.

Putting on the suit takes about forty-five minutes with the help of another astronaut. Once the suit is on, you must stay on the spacecraft and breathe pure oxygen for more than an hour until all the **nitrogen** leaves your body. The air pressure in the suit during a space walk is lower than on Earth, so nitrogen in the body can form bubbles, which may lead to pain or even death.

Modern space suits are safer and allow astronauts to do more jobs than previous suits allowed.

During launch and reentry to Earth, NASA astronauts wear an orange suit called the Advanced Crew Escape Suit. It is a pressurized suit with oxygen, drinking water, communications equipment, and cooling systems. During a space walk, astronauts wear a white space suit called the Extravehicular Mobility Unit (EMU).

The EMU has fourteen layers of material that help maintain air pressure, insulate the astronaut from extreme temperatures, and protect against radiation, particles, and potential tears. The white color reflects sunlight, keeping the astronaut cool. **Tethers** for attaching tools prevent gear from floating away.

A water bag and straw are mounted inside the suit so astronauts can drink, but they can't use the bathroom during space walks. It takes too much time to go inside the space station and get out of the suit, so astronauts wear diapers during space walks.

Advanced Crew Escape Suits include parachutes and inflatable life preservers astronauts can use in an emergency.

THE LIFE-SUPPORT BACKPACK

The EMU's backpack contains oxygen tanks, air filters, a battery, a radio, and a cooling system. The backpack also includes a device called SAFER. Astronauts connect to the ISS by a tether. If an astronaut breaks loose and floats away, he can use SAFER's small jets to fly back to the station.

Astronaut Mark C. Lee tests a SAFER unit in space above a background of clouds.

Dials and switches on the chest allow the astronaut to adjust the temperature, air pressure, and airflow inside the suit. The astronaut views the dials and switches using mirrors on the sleeves.

CHAPTER 3

MODERN SPACE GEAR

In 2014 Barry Wilmore needed a wrench, but there was a problem. He was an astronaut on board the ISS, and the station didn't have the tool he needed. He could get it from Earth, but the planet was about 250 miles (402 km) away.

Computer scientists on Earth designed the wrench on a computer and transmitted the design file to a 3D printer on the station. Layer by layer, the printer made the wrench.

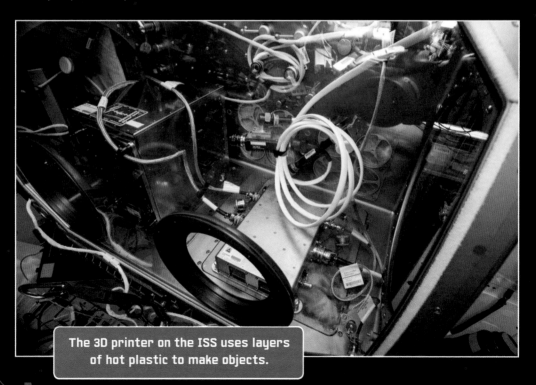

The 3D printer on the ISS uses layers of hot plastic to make objects.

Wilmore's wrench was the first tool
designed on Earth and printed in space.

Sometimes astronauts use equipment that looks like
ordinary gear, such as the wrench Wilmore needed. Other
times, they use tools specially designed for use in space,
such as the Multi-Purpose Precision Maintenance Tool.
This device has many built-in tools and a Velcro strip so
astronauts can secure it when not in use.

GEAR FOR LIVING

Astronauts sometimes use the same gear you might use on Earth. When they travel to the space station, they bring along an ordinary toothbrush, toothpaste, dental floss, and comb.

An astronaut brushes his teeth as his tube of toothpaste floats in front of him.

In 2019 astronauts had a pizza party on the ISS to celebrate a week of hard work.

Astronauts eat with regular utensils. Much of the food is **vacuum-packed**. Because plastic food containers can float away in zero gravity, astronauts attach them to trays with Velcro straps. Then they strap the tray to their lap or to a wall.

Astronauts exercise with special gear on the ISS. On Earth, gravity gives muscles and bones a daily workout. But in space, they can grow weak without gravity's pull. Astronauts use an exercise machine with stretchy bands. They run on a special treadmill by strapping a harness over their shoulders. The harness attaches to bungee cords that keep the astronaut on the machine.

Even with daily exercise, it can take astronauts months after they return to Earth to regain muscle and bone strength lost during long trips to space.

Going to the bathroom in space requires special gear too. Each astronaut has a personal attachment that fits on the body and connects to the toilet with a hose. A fan in the toilet pulls waste away from the body with air instead of water. To prevent the user from floating away, it has straps and a lap bar like the one that pulls down over your lap on a roller coaster.

CHAPTER 4

NEXT-GENERATION SPACE GEAR

At NASA's Neutral Buoyancy Laboratory in Houston, Texas, an almost full-size copy of the ISS sits at the bottom of a large, deep pool. People in space suits float nearby. They're testing how well the suits work.

It's impossible to create an environment on Earth with no gravity, but water can create a similar experience to the weightlessness of space.

Long before new types of space suits reach space, they go through testing to make sure they're safe, easy to move in, and comfortable. Since the suits must perform in an airless environment, some tests take place in a vacuum chamber, a room with almost all the air pumped out. Other tests take place in the Neutral Buoyancy Laboratory, which simulates the weightless environment of space.

Before going into space, astronauts practice every step of a space walk on Earth many times with all their gear on.

NASA's new space suits, such as the Prototype Exploration Suit, will be more comfortable and will allow astronauts to move more easily than space suits of the past.

THE FUTURE OF SPACE GEAR

NASA is designing the next generation of space gear. A new one-piece space suit for use in zero gravity, the Prototype Exploration Suit, has a hatch in the back for an astronaut to slide into. This will make it easier and faster to suit up. Another new suit, the Orion Crew Survival Systems Suit, comes with its own toilet. It's there in case astronauts can't use the toilet on the spacecraft.

NASA is designing the Z2 suit to walk on the moon or Mars. Current space suits make it difficult to bend at the waist. The Z2 is designed to be flexible enough for an astronaut to easily bend over and pick up Martian rocks.

In the future, astronauts won't need to bring all of their gear with them on space missions. They'll be able to build what they need using 3D printers. High-tech space suits and 3D-printed gear will play huge roles in future missions to the moon and Mars.

NASA plans to send astronauts to Mars in the 2030s.

Follow the links below to download 3D printer files for the Apollo 11 landing site, the Multi-Purpose Precision Maintenance Tool, and Barry Wilmore's wrench:

Apollo 11 landing site, http://qrs.lernerbooks.com/Apollo11

Multi-Purpose Precision Maintenance Tool, http://qrs.lernerbooks.com/MPMT

Wrench, http://qrs.lernerbooks.com/Wrench

air pressure: pressure created by a mass of air such as an atmosphere

carbon dioxide: an invisible, colorless gas that people exhale

nitrogen: an invisible, colorless gas that makes up most of Earth's atmosphere

pressurized: filled with air to create air pressure similar to the pressure on Earth's surface

radiation: a type of energy that moves through space and can be harmful to people

space suits: suits equipped with everything needed to survive in space for a short time

space walk: a mission that requires an astronaut to move in space outside of a spacecraft or space station

tethers: lines by which objects or people are attached to a spacecraft to prevent them from floating away

vacuum-packed: having much of the air removed to make food last longer

Aldrin, Buzz, and Marianne Dyson. *To the Moon and Back: My Apollo 11 Adventure*. Washington, DC: National Geographic Kids, 2018.

Kurtz, Kevin. *Cutting-Edge Space Tourism*. Minneapolis: Lerner Publications, 2020.

Mara, Wil. *Breakthroughs in Space Travel*. Minneapolis: Lerner Publications, 2019.

NASA: Clickable Spacesuit
https://www.nasa.gov/audience/foreducators/spacesuits/home/clickable_suit.html

NASA: Your Body in Space
https://www.nasa.gov/audience/forstudents/5-8/features/F_Your_Body_in_Space.html

NASA Space Place: Science & Technology
https://spaceplace.nasa.gov/menu/science-and-technology/

National Geographic Kids: The Moon Landing
https://kids.nationalgeographic.com/explore/history/moon-landing/

Zoehfeld, Kathleen Weidner. *Apollo 13: How Three Brave Astronauts Survived a Space Disaster*. New York: Random House, 2015.

INDEX

Photo Acknowledgments

Image credits: Freer/Shutterstock.com, p. 2 (bottom); NASA, pp. 4, 5, 6, 7, 8, 9, 10, 11, 12, 13, 14, 16, 18, 19, 21, 23; NASA/James Blair, p. 15; Robert Markowitz/NASA, p. 17; ESA, p. 20; NASA/ESA, p. 22; NASA/NBL/Bill Brassard, p. 24; Mark Sowa/NASA, p. 25; NASA/Bill Stafford, p. 26; gorodenkoff/Getty Images, p. 27; ESA/S. Corvaja, p. 28. Design elements: Jetrel/Shutterstock.com; Nanashiro/Shutterstock.com; phiseksit/Shutterstock.com; MSSA/Shutterstock.com; Pakpoom Makpan/Shutterstock.com; pixelparticle/Shutterstock.com; wacomka/Shutterstock.com; fluidworkshop/Shutterstock.com.

Cover: Vadim Sadovski/Shutterstock.com.

Lerner Publications Company
An imprint of Lerner Publishing Group, Inc.
241 First Avenue North
Minneapolis, MN USA 55401

For reading levels and more information, look up this title at www.lernerbooks.com.

Main body text set in Aptifer Sans LT Pro.
Typeface provided by Linotype AG.

Library of Congress Cataloging-in-Publication Data

The Cataloging-in-Publication Data for *Space gear in Action: An Augmented Reality Experience* is on file at the Library of Congress.
ISBN 978-1-5415-7884-5 (lib. bdg.)
ISBN 978-1-5415-8944-5 (pbk.)
ISBN 978-1-5415-8349-8 (eb pdf)

LC record available at https://lccn.loc.gov/2019020811

Manufactured in the United States of America
1-46987-47856-7/24/2019